Everything You Always Wanted to Know About Preschool — But Didn't Know Whom to Ask

by Ellen Booth Church
with Deb Matthews

Copyright © 1996 by Scholastic Inc.
Illustrations copyright © 1996 by Scholastic Inc.
All rights reserved. Published by Scholastic Inc.
Printed in the U.S.A.
ISBN 0-590-93601-8
2   3   4   5   6   7   8   9   10   02   01

Table of Contents

12. What does "developmentally appropriate" mean, and how does it apply to my preschool?

13. What is the role of play in preschool?

14. What skills will my child learn?

15. What is the role of cultural diversity in a preschool program, and how will my child's culture be reflected?

16. How can I tell if my child is being disciplined appropriately?

17. How can I assess the program's health and safety procedures?

18. How can I become involved in my child's preschool experience?

19. What is kindergarten screening all about?

20. How can I tell if my child is ready for kindergarten?

Plus ...

A (baker's) dozen things to ask your child's preschool teacher

6 things to look for in the preschool classroom

Books to share with your child

1 Why should my child go to preschool?

Preschool is not only wonderful preparation for elementary school; it's a place where young children can meet and interact, feel safe away from Mom or Dad, learn, and have fun! A quality preschool stimulates your child's imagination and physical, social, and emotional development, and provides opportunities for intellectual exploration.

In preschool, your child learns to relate to adults outside his or her own family and develop independence. Playing in a group provides your child with opportunities to learn how to share, take turns, cooperate, and solve problems. Playing with materials and participating in activities that are designed or selected specifically for young children, helps your child develop early reading, writing, science, art, math, and other skills. These activities broaden your child's experiences and are springboards for later learning.

2   What will my child learn in preschool that he or she can't learn at home?

That's a good question. Remember, *you* are your child's first teacher! Preschool experiences enhance what you are already doing to help your child learn at home.

At the same time, children benefit when they venture outside their home environments and into new territory. In the "outside world," they can encounter new people, have new experiences, and learn new things. As children begin to explore the world away from Mom or Dad, they begin to develop a budding sense of competence and independence. Preschool is designed to offer your child these opportunities in a secure, predictable environment, guided by an adult who is not only familiar and nurturing, but is also trained in helping young children learn.

3 What might a typical daily schedule look like?

A good preschool day is made up of time blocks which alternate between different kinds of activities. It is predictable so children know what to expect, but flexible to allow for special events and changing circumstances. More important than the specific times of the schedule is its underlying, unmistakable rhythm. For three- or four-year-olds, it is this rhythm, much more than the clock, that gives form to the day.

The following is a sample schedule. Naturally, individual schedules will vary, especially for programs with a shorter day. But most programs include these time blocks, or some variation of them, to provide your child with a well-rounded day.

Sample Schedule

Arrival and Greeting Time
quiet games, books, puzzles
(approximately ½ hour)

Circle Time
(approximately 15 minutes)

Activity Time
also called Choice Time
(1 – 1½ hours)

Morning Snacktime
(20 minutes)

Outdoor or Gross-Motor Play Time
(45 minutes–1 hour)

Meal Time
setting tables, eating, and clearing
(30–40 minutes)

Storytime
(20 minutes)

Nap or Rest Time
(about 2 hours)

Afternoon Snacktime
(20 minutes)

Activity Time
(30 minutes – 1 hour)

Departure Time

How many different types of preschools are there?

There are a few broad categories of preschool programs, which often overlap. The crucial differences for most parents are hours of operation, cost, and the educational and social benefits to children.

■ **CHILD-CARE** (or day-care) centers are open full-time to meet the needs of working parents.

■ **NURSERY SCHOOLS** may be part day or full day and part week or full week.

■ **FAMILY CHILD CARE,** which is licensed care that takes place in the provider's home, usually offers flexible hours.

Some programs, like Montessori preschools, are based on very specific educational philosophies. Others draw on a variety of models and learning theories. Ask the program director at any school that interests you to explain the program's philosophy and goals. Continue a dialogue even after your child is enrolled.

Locating Programs

A local resource and referral service can provide information about programs in your area. You can find the number in the telephone book, or call the National Association of Child Care Resource and Referral Agencies at (202) 393-5501.

The important news is that neither the type of program nor its cost determines the benefits a particular preschool can offer your child.

Child-care centers, nursery schools, and family child-care homes can all provide nurturing, educational environments. More expensive preschools may or may not provide better programs than less expensive ones.

5 What makes a quality preschool program?

THE TEACHERS!
Materials, facilities, safety procedures, and supportive administrators are all important, but more than anything else, the teachers make preschool a positive experience for your child.

Your child's preschool teacher should take obvious delight in children and communicate openly with parents. She should understand the developmental needs of young children in general, and build on the individual strengths of each child.

Other key elements of a quality preschool program are:

■ **HEALTH AND SAFETY**
A well-run preschool is clean and well-maintained.

Space is carefully designed, equipment is in good repair, and simple rules are established and expressed clearly to children. Adults in the school follow sound health procedures such as washing their hands routinely and handling food safely.

■ **EMOTIONAL SECURITY**
A quality preschool is a "safe zone" for feelings. Teachers demonstrate respect and understanding for children at all times. Feelings are validated verbally ("You're sad today because your friend is absent") and nonverbally (hugs and eye contact). Positive disciplinary techniques are used, such as redirecting children to more

appropriate activities. Logical consequences, rather than punishments, follow a child's behavior.

■ **A SOUND CURRICULUM**
Curriculum in quality preschools is a careful blend of teacher-initiated activities that build on children's interests, and children's self-directed activities and play. Activities are suited to children's ages and abilities, and address all areas of development: intellectual, social, emotional, physical, and creative.

6 How large should the class be?

In most preschools, you'll find groups of about 14 to 20 children for three-year-olds, and 16 to 20 children for four-year-olds. A smaller group may be fine, even advantageous, for your child. But the National Association for the Education of Young Children (NAEYC) recommends that to ensure a quality program, the class size should not exceed 20. Some states even have regulations against groups larger than 20 for preschoolers.

More important perhaps than class size is the number of teachers present. A good ratio of teachers to children means there are enough adults to run the classroom smoothly and safely, and to offer your child plenty of one-to-one attention. NAEYC recommends at least one teacher for every 10 preschoolers.

To Contact NAEYC

NAEYC is a member organization that sets professional standards and policies for early childhood education. If you are interested, you can call them for more information at (800) 424-2460.

7 How can I tell if a preschool is a good match for my child?

To decide if a school is a good match, consider your child's temperament, his or her ability to play alone and with others, and how you both feel about the teacher. It is always useful to take some time to visit the classroom and observe the teacher/child interactions. Then, after you enroll your child, stay tuned! Is your child talking happily about teachers and friends? Is she adjusting smoothly to the rhythm of the activities in the classroom?

Your child should feel connected with her teacher very soon, and have a real sense of belonging within the first few weeks. If these connections don't form, discuss your concerns with the teacher. There may be a specific problem that you can work out together. Only if your child is withdrawn or truly unhappy for an extended period, should you consider making a change. But if there's a sparkle in her eyes, you can be fairly sure you have found a good match!

8 How can I best prepare my child for his or her first school experience?

Talk with your child about his feelings related to school, friends, teachers, and new activities. Look for books on these topics and read them together. (See **Books to share with your child.**) Help your child identify some of the things he might see and do at school.

If possible, visit the classroom with your child.

In addition, you may want to invite his teacher to your home. This creates a special connection in advance between your child and his teacher.

You can also prepare your child by encouraging self-help skills such as dressing, undressing, and washing hands. Let him practice making simple choices on his own. If he is unaccustomed to playing with other children, try to make opportunities for him to do so. Practicing these skills will help your child feel confident and will smooth the way for a happy transition into preschool. After school starts, continue talking with your child about his experiences.

9 What if my child doesn't want to leave me?

It's natural for children to be concerned about starting new experiences. If your child is reacting strongly, perhaps a recent change in your family is causing some insecurity. Or perhaps your child, by nature, is a cautious person.

Your child will separate from you more easily if you express consistency, reassurance, and a willingness to let her go — even if you're feeling a little sad and nervous, too. Listen to her concerns and validate her feelings. The first few days, if possible, stay with her until she seems ready to separate. Then be *sure* you say goodbye — sneaking out may avoid an upsetting scene, but it makes your child feel even less secure. Often, it helps to create a ritual such as a hug and two waves at the door before you leave.

Once you leave, don't wave forever at the window, and don't return to be sure she's okay — you'll just have to separate all over again! If you want to, call the school later to see how she's doing. Chances are they'll be able to tell you she's just fine.

10 Beyond separation, what social and emotional challenges will my child meet in preschool, and what's the best way to handle them?

Being in a group, getting used to the variety of stimulating choices, having to wait for others before doing things — all of these can be difficult adjustments for young children. Like any group activity, preschool requires patience, flexibility, responsibility, and the ability to listen. These skills come more easily to some children than to others. And your child will react to the stress of these challenges in his own unique way.

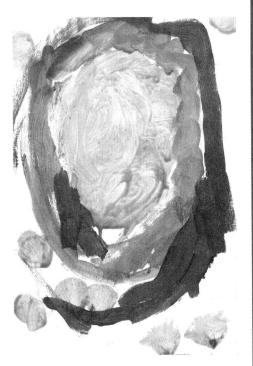

You can best help your child by staying in close contact with his teacher, helping him get plenty of rest and reassurance, and reinforcing social skills at home. Keep in mind that your child's teacher does not expect him to handle all these challenges on his own yet. Instead, she views them as skills he will develop during the preschool years. Everyone working together is the best way to support your child's growth.

What can I share with the teacher to help make this a successful year for everyone?

Share as much as you can! Take some time and write down your child's interests, likes, dislikes, special strengths, and favorite family traditions. If you can, communicate what you know about your child's temperament. Perhaps your child has a difficult time being in a large group. Maybe she is very shy around new people, or is aggressive at times. Let teachers in on this. Then, throughout the year, continue to keep teachers informed about upcoming events, a poor night's sleep, and anything else that may affect your child's behavior. Often, just knowing what to expect enables teachers to minimize conflicts and keep small problems from becoming big ones.

What does "developmentally appropriate" mean, and how does it apply to my preschool?

"Developmentally appropriate" describes an approach to teaching that respects both the age and the individual needs of each child. The idea is that the program should fit the child; the child shouldn't have to fit the program!

Preschool teachers look at the "whole child," including intellectual, social, emotional, physical, and creative growth. Of course, every child develops in these different areas at his own rate, and the range of these rates can be quite wide at any given age. A child may, for example, have strong intellectual skills and need more development socially.

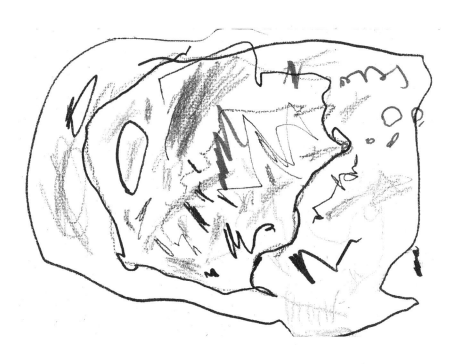

There are, however, some common developmental patterns that parents and teachers can expect to see.

Through training and/or experience, your child's teacher is familiar with these patterns. She uses this information and her observations of the group to carefully plan activities that are not too simple or too difficult, but that help each child learn and grow. Many developmentally appropriate activities are open-ended, which means they have flexible procedures and there are few right or wrong answers. This way, children at different developmental levels can participate with equal success.

How can you tell if your child's preschool is developmentally appropriate? One good way is simply to watch the children in action. If most of them seem busy and engaged in their own independent activities, rather than bored or frustrated by activities the teacher directs, the program is probably appropriate. You can also speak to the teacher or director about how the curriculum in your child's classroom meets individual needs. Finally, inquire if the program is accredited by the National Association for the Education of Young Children (NAEYC). NAEYC accreditation is your seal of approval that the program is developmentally appropriate.

13 What is the role of play in preschool?

In preschool, play is the hub of all activity. Because young children understand things when they use or experience them directly, they learn more through play than any other way. When your child plays house, paints, or builds with blocks, she is learning how to express herself, solve problems, and test out her ideas about how things work.

Good preschool classrooms are designed to encourage play. Most have a pretend- or dramatic-play area, an art area, a blocks area, a math/manipulatives area, a library, and other areas; each stocked with stimulating, hands-on materials. The daily schedule should allow plenty of time for play.

It's important for children to choose and direct their play by themselves. Teachers enhance play by offering fresh materials and suggesting new ideas at appropriate times. They should also be ready and willing to join in children's play — when they are invited!

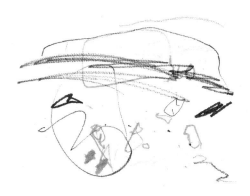

14   What skills will my child learn?

The list is almost endless. Socially, your child will begin learning to share not only toys, but also conversation, teachers' laps, and snacks. He will learn to resolve conflicts with other children; how and when to stand up for himself; and when to yield to another.

Emotionally, his self-esteem will grow as he is encouraged to do things for himself, from making decisions to setting his place for lunch.

Physically, fine-motor skills such as cutting, pasting, stapling, taping, and painting will be sharpened on a daily basis. Gross-motor skills such as running and throwing will be practiced outdoors.

Intellectually, the skills your child will learn are amazing. Opportunities to develop math and science skills such as matching, sorting, measuring, observing, and hypothesizing, will abound. Your child's imagination will grow through make-believe (dramatic) play. Language skills will grow through conversations with friends and teachers. Early reading and writing skills will develop as he looks at books, paints at the easel, writes letters to his friends, and has countless other experiences with print.

15 What is the role of cultural diversity in a preschool program, and how will my child's culture be reflected?

Even three- and four-year-olds are tuned in to matters of culture and ethnicity. For them, the issues are not social but personal, and are closely related to their self-esteem. They want to know, "Am I valued here?" When their races, cultural heritages, and families are respected and reflected in the classroom, children can begin to feel that they belong.

If your child's preschool validates cultural diversity, you'll know it just by looking around. Are a variety of faces represented on the walls? Do the materials and activities reflect the cultures of the children in the room, and other cultures as well? Notice what aspects of children's cultures are included in classroom displays and discussions; and in books, materials, games, music, and even food prepared for lunch or snack. Remember that *culture* is not only about race or nationality, but is also rooted in family traditions. Find ways to contribute aspects of your family's heritage to your child's classroom to enrich the learning experience for all.

"We are all alike and different" is an important concept in the preschool curriculum. Activities that teach about similarities and differences in realistic, positive ways help your child value and respect herself, and others as well.

16 How can I tell if my child is being disciplined appropriately?

Your preschool should have a written policy that lets you know clearly what kinds of discipline techniques are used in classrooms. For an even better feel, ask the teacher or director to tell you how a specific situation would be handled in the classroom.

In any preschool program, corporal punishment should be strictly forbidden. Also, teachers should never shame or ridicule a child. Instead, *redirecting* — which helps a child focus on what *is* allowed rather than what *isn't* — should be used to channel energy and curiosity. Teachers should point out the logical consequences of children's actions and follow through with caring but firm limits.

How teachers communicate with children is an important point in any discussion about discipline. Do teachers make their expectations clear? Are respect and understanding evident in tone and body language? Teachers should neither talk down to children nor heap on excessive, insincere praise. Methods that empower children to articulate their thoughts and feelings build self-esteem and are the best forms of preventive discipline.

"A person"

17 How can I assess the program's health and safety procedures?

While it's normal for children in preschool to get sick sometimes or get occasional bumps and bruises, as a parent you should feel satisfied that your child's preschool is following sound health and safety procedures.

Your state is responsible for setting and monitoring minimum health and safety standards in preschools. The preschool should have available written information describing health and safety policies and procedures and how they affect your child.

If you want to check firsthand that policies are being implemented, the best way is to notice what happens in the classroom.

Look for teachers washing their hands thoroughly and often. Note if they actively observe children on indoor and outdoor play structures. Also, ask questions. How often are toys and tabletops cleaned? How would the program communicate with you in the event of a contagious disease? Are fire drills held regularly?

If you have any concerns about procedures, discuss them with your child's teacher or the program director.

18 How can I become involved in my child's preschool experience?

Preschool teachers should welcome your interest and encourage you to participate in the program in a variety of ways. In addition to talking with each other frequently about your child, here are a few ways to get involved that will help create a meaningful parent-teacher relationship:

■ **VOLUNTEER IN THE CLASSROOM!** Moms and dads (and other family members) who assist in preschools have the pleasure of seeing all the fun, growing, and learning that goes on firsthand.

■ **SHARE A SPECIAL SKILL** or family tradition with your child's class. Perhaps you can play an instrument, make toys from wood, or do a special kind of weaving. Or maybe you just love reading stories to an appreciative audience. When you share yourself and your family, everyone's preschool experience will be enriched.

- **KEEP A NOTEBOOK** of your child's development or special anecdotes the way teachers often do. Share your notes with his teacher informally and during parent-teacher conferences. Your notebook will help you see your child's many accomplishments throughout the year!

- **TRY A NEW WAY OF RECYCLING.** Teachers can almost always use discarded materials such as plastic containers, spools, paper-towel tubes, old greeting cards, wrapping paper, dress-up clothes, and even used small appliances.

- **STAY IN TOUCH WITH YOUR CHILD'S TEACHER TO FIND OUT WHAT SHE NEEDS.**

In addition to these suggestions, many preschools want or even require parents to participate in fundraisers or occasional "cleanup" days, to serve on advisory boards, and so on. Whatever ways you choose, try to make time to get involved. You — and your child — will be glad you did!

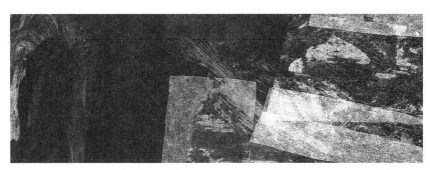

19 What is kindergarten screening all about?

Screening helps prospective kindergarten teachers learn a little bit about their future students. It is a one-time evaluation, usually administered in late spring. Kindergarten screening focuses mainly on cognitive and physical skill levels, and is designed to help determine what your child's abilities and needs are in these areas. Teachers can and should use screening as a tool to begin planning the best ways to work with your child.

Unfortunately, teachers and parents often view screening as a conclusive test that shows whether or not a child is ready for kindergarten. But screenings are only one small piece of your child's developmental profile. Direct observations of your child by her prospective kindergarten teacher, assessments by her preschool teacher, *your opinion* of her skills, and in some cases, evaluations by doctors or other specialists, should all be considered.

20 How can I tell if my child is ready for kindergarten?

The real question is: "Is this kindergarten ready for my child?"

Ideally, every kindergarten should be able to respond to each child's individual needs.

Realistically, however, some programs may not be as developmentally appropriate as others. If your child's fifth birthday falls near the cutoff date for school admission, or if he seems particularly immature

compared with others his age, you may want to consider whether the school is ready to meet his needs.

Talk with educators in your community about the kindergarten curriculum in relation to your child's motor skills, language abilities, and social needs. Discuss how he interacts with large groups, and how he is progressing with self-help and fine-motor skills. Find out how the kindergarten will accommodate itself to support your child. Only then consider whether he might benefit from waiting one more year.

If for some reason your child is not ready for kindergarten, it's important that neither you nor he feel like you've failed. Most five-year-olds have a wonderful capacity for learning and growing. Nurture your child's excitement and, together, look ahead with joyous anticipation to the next learning experience!

A (baker's) dozen
things to ask
your child's preschool teacher

1. What will a typical day be like for my child?

2. How many children are in the class?
How many adults will assist in the program?

3. What is your experience teaching preschool?
What kind of training have you had?

4. How can I help my child feel comfortable separating from
me during the first few weeks?

5. If my child has problems adjusting or needs extra help, how
will you let me know so I can be part of the solution?

6. What happens if my child has a conflict with another child?
How will you handle it?

7. What is your approach to discipline in the classroom?

8. Is there a handbook with information concerning school
policies on discipline, health and safety, emergency
procedures, school closings, and parent involvement?

9. How much time will my child be spending outdoors? What is your foul weather policy?

10. When should I keep my child home? What happens if my child gets sick at school?

11. What can I do at home to support what my child learns in school?

12. What's the best way for us to create a supportive parent-teacher relationship? How can we keep in touch with each other?

13. Do you have an "open door" policy? What are some ways for me to volunteer in the classroom or program?

6 things to look
for in the
preschool classroom

1. Is there enough indoor space for children to move freely? Can children easily work and play alone or in small groups? Is the room clean and well-maintained?

2. Are toys and materials within children's reach? Are shelves and containers labeled so children know where to find things and put them away?

3. Is children's artwork celebrated and displayed at children's eye level?

4. Is cultural diversity evident in photos, posters, literature, and dramatic-play props?

5. Is the play yard safe, yet challenging? Does it contain age-appropriate equipment?

6. Is the teacher having a good time? Is she playfully and meaningfully interacting with children? Does she make you and the children feel welcome?